THE POWER O

A Stoic's Guide to Unyielding Focus

KEVIN L. MICHEL

THE POWER OF THE PRESENT: A Stoic's Guide to Unyielding Focus

Names: Michel, Kevin L.
Title: The Power of the Present: A Stoic's Guide to Unyielding Focus
Subjects: Stoicism, Personal Growth, Success, Goals

For information regarding permissions,
write to: KevinLMichel@gmail.com

www.KevinMichel.com

CONTENTS

INTRODUCTION
The Distracting World

Just as the sun is forever pursued by shadows, so too is our purpose chased by an unending flurry of distractions. They are the specters of our existence, conjured by the ceaseless clatter of the world, whispering tales of urgency and importance that often bear no relevance to our true path.

In this grand theatre we call life, distractions play their parts convincingly. They adorn themselves in the grandeur of the immediate, urgent, and superficial, dazzling our senses and demanding our attention. They leap into the spotlight, shouting loudly to drown the quiet callings of our deepest intentions.

These distractions are akin to the relentless waves of the ocean, crashing against the shores of our consciousness. They erode our resolve, and little by little, wash away the sandcastles of our focus. They arrive in various guises: the allure of trivial pleasures, the lure of the inconsequential, the din of idle gossip, the chains of past regret and the ghostly shadows of future anxieties. Each wave seeks to pull us into the depths of irrelevance, away from the firm ground of meaningful pursuits.

Yet, amidst this tempestuous sea, our dreams reside, like a distant lighthouse, steadfast and patient. They wait for us to navigate the storm, to steer our ship through the crashing waves and reach the tranquility of focused intent. The challenge, therefore, is not to calm the sea, but to become skilled mariners, to learn to sail even in the fiercest storm. Indeed, distractions are not the enemy, but the terrain we must traverse. They form the tumultuous backdrop against which the drama of life unfolds. It is within this cacophonous symphony that we must learn to discern the melody of our purpose, to heed its call, and to dance to its rhythm.

Distractions are the tests we must pass, the dragons we must slay on our quest. They serve as reminders, sharpening our understanding of what truly deserves our focus. Every moment we choose to ignore their siren call, we strengthen our resolve, we fortify our castle of focus against the unrelenting tide.

Our task, then, is not to fear the distracting world, but to learn to thrive within it, to become the eye of the storm, calm amidst chaos. To be like the oak that stands tall against the howling winds, not because it is immune to the storm, but because it has learned to weather it. Such is the power of an unyielding focus in a world beset by distractions.

The Stoic's path is akin to walking against the gusts of a tempest, unswayed and unbroken. As pilgrims in this grand spectacle of existence, we are not immune to the winds of the world. Yet, we may choose to remain unwavering, bearing the brunt of the gusts with equanimity. This is the Stoic's virtue.

At its core, Stoicism, like the sturdy oak tree, stands firm amidst the torrential downpour of life's distractions. It teaches us that while we may not command the winds to change, we possess the power to adjust our sails, to guide our minds through the tumultuous sea of life's happenings.

Stoicism, like a seasoned sculptor, fashions the raw marble of our attention into a well-honed pillar of focus. The true currency of our existence is not time, but attention. The past and the future are but shadows and specters that have no claim over the vivacious vitality of the present moment. Stoicism implores us to dispense our attention wisely, not on the ephemeral apparitions of past regrets or future anxieties, but on the solid ground of the present.

In this practice of presence, the Stoic finds serenity. The world might rage around, yet within the Stoic's mind, a tranquil sea prevails. The Stoic remains anchored, not carried away by the torrents of distraction, but rather cultivating a steadfast presence in each fleeting moment. In this ever-passing instant, the Stoic exercises his virtue, sharpens his wisdom, and wields his actions.

Thus, Stoicism offers us a compass and a rudder, guiding us towards focus and presence. In the ceaseless ebb and flow of existence, it provides the principles to steer our minds towards the harbors of tranquility and purposeful action. The Stoic approach is the lighthouse that guides us amidst the tempest, leading us to the land of dreams crafted in the forge of the unyielding present.

CHAPTER 1: THE NATURE OF FOCUS

The mind is a prolific explorer, ever-wandering. It saunters through ancient ruins of regrets, climbs the lofty peaks of ambition, and meanders through the untrodden paths of uncertainty. However, it is in the quiet valley of the present that the mind must make its home if it is to truly understand the nature of focus.

The act of focusing is not simply the mental equivalent of gazing intently at an object. It is a confluence, a harmonious marriage of mind, heart, and will, an alignment akin to a troupe of actors on a stage, each playing their part, but all moving in harmony towards the climax of the play. This is the essence of true focus.

Yet the object of our focus is not to be chosen lightly. In the marketplace of ambitions, dreams are sold in all sizes and shapes. But true fulfillment and achievement do not lie in the mere attainment of goals, but rather in the pursuit of those that are truly worthy. A target, after all, gives direction to our arrow, but the archer's glory lies not in merely hitting the target, but in striking one that demands skill and character.

Beware the folly of lending your focus to vain pursuits. Just as a river, when it is split into countless rivulets, loses its force and becomes but a whimper, a mind divided by trivial pursuits dissipates its strength. Focus, therefore, is not merely concentration, it is selection; not merely observation, it is dedication.

But do not mistake this call to focus as an invitation to a state of perpetual mental strain. Just as a bow, if always strung taut, loses its strength, so too does a mind unyieldingly strained lose its resilience. True focus is the ability to summon our mental strength when it is required and to let it rest when it is not.

Imagine, if you will, a bird in flight. When it must overcome the gusts that hinder its path, it beats its wings with unyielding force. Yet, when it soars high in the sky, it spreads its wings and rides the wind, at peace in its journey. This is the model of focus we must aspire to: resolute in the face of opposition, tranquil in the embrace of flow.

Thus, true focus requires wisdom in choosing the worthy target, courage in maintaining a resolute mind, and prudence in knowing when to exert effort and when to seek rest. Master these elements, and you begin to understand the nature of focus. Armed with this understanding, you can navigate the vast seas of distraction and stay the course towards the island of your dreams.

The mind can be viewed as a seasoned traveler, ceaselessly journeying on the winding roads of time. Eternally restless, it seldom finds reprieve in the haven of the present, instead meandering between the relics of the past and the prospects of the future. This is the wanderer mind, forever a stranger to the peace of the now.

To understand the nature of this relentless wanderer, one must fathom its ceaseless quest. When our thoughts turn towards the past, we are often mired in the seductive trap of regret or bathed in the illusory glow of nostalgia. We wallow in the murky waters of what once was, reaching out to the shadows of deeds done and words uttered. Yet, the past is but a deserted stage, the actors long departed, the play concluded. No amount of wandering in its hallowed halls can change the script that was once performed.

Equally enticing is the shimmering allure of the future. Our mind, much like an eager seafarer, sets sail to the distant horizon, hoping to catch a glimpse of what is yet to come. In this endless expanse, we construct castles of aspirations and paint portraits of dread, weaving a tapestry of anticipation that exists nowhere but within the confines of our thoughts. The future, though yet unwritten, becomes a siren's song that pulls us away from the shore of the present.

Yet, both past and future are but illusions, mere phantoms birthed by the wanderer mind. They are echoes and whispers, devoid of the tangible solidity of the present moment. We become the masters of time, not by traversing its illusory breadth, but by plunging into the depth of the present moment.

In the now, the wanderer mind finds a purpose. Like a wayward ship finally dropping anchor in a tranquil bay, it experiences respite. The now, the simple reality of what is, serves as a beacon, illuminating the path for the wanderer. When the mind ceases to roam and learns to reside in the present, it finds itself not in a barren wasteland, but in a fertile ground where the seeds of intention can be sown, where the fruits of action can be reaped.

Therefore, we must seek to tame this wanderer mind, not by chaining it to the immovable past or the unarrivable future, but by inviting it to rest in the embrace of the present moment. For in the now lies the true journey's end of the wanderer, a place where dreams take root, grow, and flourish. The past has had its turn, the future will have its time, but the stage belongs to the present. It is here, and nowhere else, that the drama of life unfolds.

THE PILLARS OF FOCUS: CLARITY, INTENTION, AND PERSEVERANCE

Just as the mighty edifice requires a firm foundation to withstand the trials of time and tempest, our focus too rests upon three essential pillars: clarity, intention, and perseverance. Together, they form the bedrock of our purposeful existence, lending strength and direction to our pursuits.

Clarity, the first pillar, is the light that illuminates our path. It is the crystal stream that cuts through the overgrowth of confusion, revealing the truth of our course. Without clarity, we are but wanderers in the labyrinth of existence, prone to the alluring whispers of distractions. To cultivate clarity is to cast a beacon upon the landscape of our minds, exposing distractions for what they truly are: phantom echoes of an unfocused mind.

Next is Intention, the compass of our journey. Our intentions act as the rudder of our ship, guiding us unerringly towards our chosen destination amidst the turbulent seas of life. Without intention, our actions are as aimless as the leaf adrift on the wind, susceptible to the faintest of gusts. To anchor ourselves in intention is to tether our will to our purpose, providing steadfast direction in the storm of distractions.

Lastly, we turn to Perseverance, the unwavering resolve that fuels our journey. It is the echo of our footsteps on the path of purpose, never ceasing, always pressing forward. Without perseverance, our resolve crumbles at the first encounter with adversity, allowing distractions to veer us off course. To strengthen our perseverance is to forge an invincible spirit, undeterred by the seductive calls of distractions.

Imagine, if you will, an archer. His clarity is seen in the choice of the target, the intention is his decision to release the arrow, and perseverance is reflected in his steady hand and unwavering gaze as he aligns the shot, notwithstanding the distractions around him. It is this harmonious alignment of clarity, intention, and perseverance that ensures the arrow finds its mark. Similarly, these are the very elements that channel our energies towards the attainment of our dreams.

Thus, as we journey forward, let us ground our focus on these three pillars. Let our clarity dispel the fog of distractions, our intention steer us forward, and our perseverance propel us against the currents of adversity. With these pillars firmly within our grasp, we become masters of our journey, captains of our own ship, no longer at the mercy of the whispering winds of distraction.

THE MISUNDERSTOOD TARGET

Myriad stars twinkle in the night sky, each a potential destination for the wanderer. But not all stars hold the same allure, and not all lead to a journey of fulfillment. This is the dilemma of choice, and the art of selecting our focus. We may find ourselves gazing in wonder at the entire constellation, yet, it is only when we pick a singular star to guide us that we truly embark on our voyage.

Focus is not merely a compass, pointing in a fixed direction, but rather an unwavering commitment to a chosen destination. This is the arrow of intention, pulled back on the bowstring of the mind, aimed at a target worthy of pursuit. The common misunderstanding lies in believing that any target will suffice. This is not so. The trivial may distract and the transient may deceive, leading one on a course towards fleeting satisfaction and inevitable regret. No, the target of our focus must be meaningful, a lodestar that aligns with our deepest values and noblest aspirations.

Much like a gardener does not water every seed indiscriminately, but chooses those that promise to bloom into magnificent flowers, we too must discern the seeds of our dreams. Our time, our energy, our attention - these are precious resources that must be allocated not merely to what sparkles, but to what endures.

Think of the towering oak, its acorn was once buried in the darkness of the earth, forgotten by all. Yet it was chosen. The attention of the sun, the nourishment of the rain, all were directed towards this small, seemingly insignificant seed. Their focus was not swayed by the myriad other elements, but was steady and unchanging. And in time, the acorn bloomed into a majestic oak, its roots deep in the earth and branches high in the sky.

Remember, a meaningful target is not always the most ostentatious, nor is it the easiest to achieve. But it is the one that aligns with your true self, resonates with your deepest core. Such a target is like a song that, once heard, echoes in the chambers of the heart, stirring within us the courage to venture towards its melody. It transcends the mundane, reaching out to the realms of the extraordinary.

Therefore, let not your focus be waylaid by the glittering distractions of the world. Select a target that is worthy of your pursuit, that aligns with your soul's yearning. Do this, and the arrow of your focus will fly true, cutting through the noise of the world, and finding its mark in the realm of purpose and fulfillment. Let your chosen star guide your journey, illuminating your path even in the deepest of nights, and anchoring your voyage in the harbor of profound meaning.

CHAPTER 2: THE FOLLY OF TIME-TRAVEL

The human mind is an expert time-traveler. It roams the vast expanse of time, often departing the present's shores, navigating the murky waters of the past or venturing into the stormy seas of the future. Yet, this ceaseless voyaging brings no honor to our hearts, nor wisdom to our minds. For such travels cast shadows of regret and worry, shrouding the clarity of the present moment in unnecessary fog.

The Irrevocable Past

When we voyage through the seas of life, it is the present moment that serves as our ship, the future, our uncharted destination, and the past, the distant shore from which we've set sail. To dwell on the past is akin to attempting to navigate our vessel using shores that have long since faded from view.

The past, immutable and unyielding, is a book whose pages have been written, sealed by the relentless march of time. Just as an artist cannot alter the strokes of a brush once they have met the canvas, we too cannot change the actions and decisions that now reside in the realm of memory. This is the irrevocable nature of the past.

To linger in the past is to become lost in a labyrinth of echo and shadow, where each turn only leads deeper into the realm of what once was. What profit is there in wandering through these abandoned halls? Does the farmer sow seeds in a field already harvested? To dwell in the past is to till a barren field, hoping in vain for a harvest that will never come.

Our minds may find solace in revisiting old joys, or perhaps seek lessons in the remembrance of past follies. Yet, the comfort of nostalgic joy can too easily turn into a yearning for times forever lost, and the useful contemplation of past mistakes may darken into the fruitless torment of regret. Balance, as in all things, is key. While we may visit the past, we must guard against taking up permanent residence there.

Understand, dear reader, that the past serves as a reference, not a residence. A guidepost, not a destination. It is a mirror in which we may see the reflection of who we once were, but we must remember that we live in the world of the living, not in the reflection of a mirror. Life, like a river, flows always forward. Let us then, like the river, move ceaselessly towards the future, with our eyes firmly fixed on the ever-unfolding present.

In essence, we must learn to sail on the winds of the present, leaving the immutable shores of the past behind us. In this act of releasing the unchangeable, we unburden our minds, enabling ourselves to experience fully the infinite possibilities of the now. In this, we find our freedom, unchained from the specter of what was, ready to dance with the vibrant reality of what is.

THE UNCERTAIN FUTURE

From the ceaseless, winding river of time springs forth the concept we label as 'future'. A realm untrodden, it remains hidden, shrouded in the cloak of tomorrow. The future, by its very nature, is a vast canvas of uncertainty, offering an endless expanse of possibilities. Many of us, seeking control, spend our waking hours trying to foretell its fickle course, peering into this nebulous void in search of reassurance. Yet, this restless gazing into the distance often breeds not tranquility, but the seeds of anxiety.

Why do we dread the uncertain future? Because in our minds, it becomes a vessel for every conceivable calamity, every unrealized fear. It is a realm where ghostly specters of potential failures, loss, and disappointment dance. They remain just out of reach, too distant to grapple with, yet close enough to instill unease. In seeking to conquer the future, we allow it to conquer us. We become like a ship lost in fog, ever fearful of unseen rocks that might lie ahead.

However, we must remember that the ship does not fear what it cannot see, for it is simply an object, moved by the forces of nature. It is the mariner who trembles, the mind that creates specters in the fog. Yet, the mariner has a compass and a helm; tools to navigate, even in uncertainty. So too do we possess tools - wisdom, reason, courage - to navigate the unfathomable sea of future events.

Consider the farmer, who sows his seeds under the nurturing sun. He does not distress over the uncertain weather of tomorrow, nor does he agonize over the crop that is yet to grow. He simply does what is within his power: he tills the soil, he plants the seed, he waters the field. The farmer knows well that the seeds of now are the fruits of the future. He embodies the wisdom of being in the present.

Our mind is such a field, and our thoughts and actions, the seeds. The harvest is not to be demanded from the future, but nurtured in the present. We must till our minds with reason, water it with virtue, and let the sunlight of wisdom nourish it. In such preparedness, the future ceases to be a haunting specter, but becomes a friend, an ally, a natural progression of the seeds we sow today.

It is only when we abandon the futile attempt to wrestle with the uncertain future, and instead, embrace the certainty of the present, that we will find tranquility. Like the farmer, we must tend to our actions in the now, leaving the outcomes to the grand mechanism of existence. This is not a call to inaction, but a directive to relocate the locus of our concerns. The future, as vast and as mysterious as it may seem, is but a series of presents, waiting to unfold.

Thus, recognize the speculative nature of the future and understand the anxiety it brings. But do not dwell there. Instead, bring your focus back to the helm of the present. For it is here, and only here, where the waters of time can be navigated. The uncertainty of the future is but a reflection of the richness of possibility. In this truth, find not apprehension, but the freedom to sow today the seeds of tomorrow's tranquility.

In this existence, we stand at a peculiar crossroads, where the echoes of the past and the whispers of the future meet. And here, at this juncture, lies a fertile valley largely unnoticed: the present. To dwell in this valley, to till its soil, and to harvest its fruit is the pursuit of wisdom.

The past, a realm of faded spectres and echoic words, holds no power over us, save what we grant it. Like the sun setting on a distant shore, it casts long shadows that stretch into our today, but it remains removed, unreachable. The future, on the other hand, shrouded in the mist of what is yet to come, lures us with the seductive promise of control. Like the gambler who, with bated breath, watches the spinning wheel, we too await the uncertain outcome of tomorrow.

Yet the past is a silent monument, and the future, an unborn possibility. Both are beyond the dominion of our will. They are like the distant mountains that frame a landscape: while they may provide a sense of context, they are not where life is lived. Our true power does not reside in the distant shadows of what was or in the hazy light of what may come, but in the bright clarity of the present.

The present, unlike its temporal brethren, is a lively marketplace of action. Here, in this bustling agora of the now, the currency is choice, and every moment provides a fresh opportunity for transaction. We barter with existence, trading actions for outcomes, decisions for destiny. This exchange is not deferred to the unchangeable past or the unpredictable future. It happens here, in the ceaseless current of the present.

Think of the skilled potter, who shapes the wet clay not by lamenting the form it once held or by dreaming of its final shape, but by guiding his hands in the present moment, feeling the clay yield under his deft touch. His power is not in the clay's history or future, but in the interaction of the now. His attention, honed to the pressing moment, guides the clay into becoming.

So it is with our lives. Each moment is a lump of shapeless clay waiting for the artisan's hand. And we are the artisans. When we turn the wheel of our focus, we begin to see the potential of the present moment. The possibilities it holds are as boundless as the potter's artistry. Here, in the intimate interaction with the now, we find our true power.

Why, then, are we enticed by the mirage of the past and the chimera of the future? They are but shadows and fog, holding no substance for our eager hands. We are like the man who stands at the edge of a field ripe for harvest yet dreams of bygone planting seasons and future feasts. The fruit of existence is before him, ready to be plucked in the now, yet he starves amidst the bounty.

Let us not starve. Let us feast on the present moment with the appetite of those who know the taste of now. Therein lies our power: the power to choose, to act, to shape our destiny. The past is a memory, the future a mystery, but the present is a gift, a vibrant canvas awaiting the bold strokes of our focus. Like the river that carves the canyon, let us wield our power in the present, shaping the landscape of our lives with the persistent flow of now.

So let us turn our gaze from the distracting spectacles of yesterday and tomorrow, and focus on the lively play unfolding on the stage of the present. Let us embrace the power of the present, for it is the fertile soil in which the seeds of our dreams take root and bloom into the vibrant flowers of actuality.

CHAPTER 3: THE BEAUTY OF NOW

As we continue this journey, we venture now into the tranquil heart of our discourse, a serene sanctuary where time itself seems to pause: the sublime realm of the present.

In the grand theatre of time, the present stands as a solitary spotlight amidst the darkened echoes of past and the hazy projections of the future. A fleeting sliver of reality, it may seem insignificant at first glance, but it is in truth the only stage where the drama of life truly unfolds.

Consider a majestic river, its waters flowing ceaselessly, shaped by unseen forces, mirroring the march of time. Though we can peer into its depths and discern the faint reflection of what has been, and conjecture about the course it might eventually take, it is the water that passes before us in this very moment, under the bridge of our immediate perception, that is most real, most tangible.

The same applies to our lives. The past is a phantom echo, the future a mirage yet to materialize, but the present -

oh, the present is the living, breathing entity where we exist, where we act, where we can shape and be shaped.

This is the beauty of now, a fleeting yet powerful moment, a moving canvas upon which we paint the strokes of our life's art. It holds a potent charm, offering both the brush of action and the palette of experience.

Therefore, in this chapter, we shall delve into this boundless reservoir of the present moment. We shall strive to harness its power, learning to live in the richness of its depth, and to find, in its transient nature, a wellspring of purpose, peace, and presence.

The beauty of now is not hidden; it is only obscured by our neglect. It is time we clear the mist of distraction and truly behold it, for within its realm lies the key to an unyielding focus and thus, the unfolding of our grandest dreams.

The stage of life is set in the theater of the present, where the actors of the past and future play but shadows of reality. The main character, the moment of 'now', is often upstaged by these illusions, beguiling as they may be with their elaborate costumes of regrets and fantasies. Yet, within the spotlight of our attention, the true performance of life unfolds. This is the grand spectacle of the present, the embodiment of mindfulness.

Consider the river. It doesn't mull over the ground it has already covered, nor does it dread the distance it is yet to traverse. It exists solely in the present, carving its path, moment by moment, with unwavering commitment. It is entirely engaged with the 'now', shaping its journey in the ceaseless flow of water against rock, a fluid ballet of existence.

Much like the river, we too ought to embrace this ceaseless flow of existence. The present is our most loyal companion, always with us, yet so frequently overlooked. It patiently waits for us to return from our futile expeditions into the arid deserts of yesterday and the hazy jungles of tomorrow. To live in the moment is to sit by this companion, to engage in earnest conversation, and to appreciate its unvarnished reality.

Just as a master archer pulls his arrow back on the bowstring, his eyes trained on the target, his mind emptied of all but the task at hand, we too must learn to bring the entire force of our being to the fulcrum of the present. The arrow of our awareness must be pulled from the quiver of distraction and aimed solely at the target of the present. The master archer understands that the arrow can only be shot in the present, and so it is with us. Our actions, our decisions, our life - all are sculpted in the present.

This act of complete immersion in the 'now', of tuning our senses to the subtle symphony of the present moment, is the essence of mindfulness. It is an intimate dance with reality, untouched by the gaudy embellishments of the past and future. To be mindful is to strip away the unnecessary layers of abstraction, to bask in the simplicity of the moment, to truly live.

We are the sculptors of our existence, and the present is our marble. As we chip away at this block of time with the chisel of our attention, a form begins to emerge. The shape it takes depends on our mindfulness, our engagement with the present. This work cannot be done in the past, for the marble there has already been sculpted. It cannot be done in the future, for the marble there is yet unformed.

We must lay down the burdens of our past and the anticipations of our future, if only for a moment, and attend to the task at hand. Let us tune our minds to the rhythm of the present, and dance to this eternal beat. This is the path to mindfulness, to living in the moment, a path walked not in the shadows of what was or what might be, but in the radiant light of the ever-unfolding 'now'.

Consider, for a moment, the tree standing tall amidst the hallowed forest. Its roots dig deep into the fertile soil, a vast network of silent strength that grants it steadfastness against the capricious winds. The tree does not shun the present, seeking solace in the memory of past sunlight or the promise of future rains. It exists purely in the now, firm in its place, open to the sky.

This humble arboreal sentinel, standing tall through the whirlwinds of seasons, offers us a lesson in being present, in existing firmly within the confines of the current moment. A tree cannot uproot itself to escape the harshness of winter nor can it hasten the arrival of spring. It simply exists in the moment, yielding to the flow of time and nature. Each leaf that unfurls, each root that burrows further into the earth, speaks of the tree's acceptance of its present state.

In much the same way, we too should draw strength from the nourishing soil of our present circumstances, our roots reaching deep into the fertile ground of the now. The past, though filled with lessons, is a ghostly echo, its hold on us existing only within the confines of our mind. The future, on the other hand, is a spectral mirage, forever retreating over the horizon, ever beckoning but never arriving.

Bearing witness to the state of things as they are in this very moment is the first step towards true understanding. The harsh winds of adversity, the warming sunlight of prosperity, these are but temporary states. They come and go, just as winter gives way to spring, and summer gives way to autumn.

It is in the acceptance of this immutable law of nature that our understanding of presence deepens. No storm, no matter how fierce, lasts forever. No summer, no matter how bright, can stave off the eventual arrival of autumn. We are but travelers in the temporal landscape, our voyage dictated by the silent ticking of the cosmic clock.

When we anchor ourselves firmly in the present, just as the tree is anchored in the soil, we create a sense of internal stability. This stability allows us to weather life's inevitable storms with equanimity. Just as the tree bends with the wind, understanding that resistance is futile and acceptance is strength, so too must we learn to bend with the varying winds of our circumstances. Our resilience is not born of resistance to change, but acceptance of it.

Distractions may entice us with the shimmering allure of a different place or a different time. But our power, much like the tree's, lies in our ability to stay rooted in the here and now. The ability to accept and engage with the present moment, without seeking to alter it, or escape from it, is the hallmark of the rooted existence. It is through such an existence that we can draw from the wellspring of wisdom that is life itself.

Let us learn, then, from the quiet wisdom of the tree. Standing tall, deeply rooted, living entirely within the moment. It is not swayed by the whispering winds of yesterday or the echoing promises of tomorrow. It is here, now. And so, dear friend, should we strive to be. Let us become firmly rooted in the present, for it is the fertile soil in which the blossoms of wisdom and tranquility bloom.

THE CRUCIBLE OF CREATION

Each moment that arises is akin to a fiery crucible, within which we may forge the iron of our will into the steel of our reality. As an experienced blacksmith uses the heat of his furnace to transform raw ore into tools of purpose, so do we, with the forge of the present, shape our existence.

Life, as it presents itself, is raw material, no different than the iron ore in the blacksmith's hands. It is formless, without purpose, until acted upon. Just as the blacksmith would be foolish to lament the formless nature of the raw iron, we too err when we decry the nature of life's trials and tribulations.

Is it not the blacksmith's craft to shape iron? Is it not ours to shape life?

The forge's fire, in the blacksmith's workshop, is not a thing of gentle warmth. It is fierce, scorching, and unyielding. So too is the present moment. It brings with it pain, struggle, and difficulty. But remember, it is in the crucible's intense heat that the iron is made malleable, that it may be shaped and formed to the blacksmith's will.

Similarly, it is within the challenges and trials of the

present that we find our lives rendered malleable, that we may shape them according to our will. Distractions, like cold air, seek to cool the iron, rendering it rigid and unworkable. We must shield our crucible from these winds, maintaining the heat that allows for transformation.

We may liken our focus to the blacksmith's hammer, shaping the iron upon the anvil of the present. Each focused thought, each mindful action, is a stroke of that hammer, slowly but surely forging our reality.

Yet, the blacksmith does not simply strike without thought or direction. Each hammer's fall is precise, deliberate. He does not allow his mind to wander to past mistakes, to flawed creations of his former self. Nor does he give heed to future anxieties, to the looming specter of a displeased patron or the potential for failure in his creation. His mind, his focus, is in the present, with each fall of the hammer.

So it is with us. We must not be enslaved by past failures or future uncertainties. We are the blacksmiths of our existence, shaping life upon the anvil of the present. Each moment, each strike, is an opportunity for creation, for transformation. To be distracted is to miss the mark, to mar our creation.

We must then take heart, for the power to shape our existence is in our hands. It is not to be found in the quiet echoes of the past nor the whispering shadows of the future, but in the deafening roar of the present.

Indeed, the crucible of creation is not a place of gentle warmth. It is hot, fierce, demanding. But it is in this crucible, with the hammer of focus and the anvil of the present, that the shapeless iron of life is forged into the splendid steel of our dreams. Take heart, then, and welcome the heat. Embrace it, for it is the crucible of your creation.

CHAPTER 4: THE SILENT SEA WITHIN

There exists a parallel universe, as vast, mysterious, and deep as the uncharted waters of an endless sea. This universe is none other than the expanse of our inner life, hidden from the gaze of others, yet affecting our every thought, word, and action.

We navigate daily through the tumultuous waves of external stimuli, bombarded with ceaseless chatter, images, and demands. Yet, unbeknownst to us, there is another voyage that calls for our attention: the journey into the silent sea within.

Imagine, if you will, a humble shepherd's hut, enveloped in the calmness of a moonlit night. Amidst the echoes of crickets and the hushed whispers of the wind, a profound silence resonates. This tranquility is not defined by the absence of noise but is an entity in itself - a testament to the existence of quiet strength and peace. In the same manner, the silent sea within is not the absence of thoughts or feelings, but the presence of a profound stillness, a harbor amidst the tempest, a refuge that whispers, "Here, you are anchored."

Why do we sail these waters, you may ask? The answer,

dear reader, is as simple as it is profound. The journey inward is a voyage towards self-mastery. As we navigate the silent sea within, we learn to distinguish the eddies and currents of our thoughts, emotions, and desires. In this understanding, we gain a rudder to steer our lives more skillfully.

Within these depths, we find not an echo of the world's noise, but the resounding voice of our own purpose. The art of sailing this sea does not lie in evading the external tempests of life. No, it demands a far greater courage: to brave the internal storms, to hear the hushed whispers of our genuine self, and to heed its guidance.

In this chapter, we explore this silent sea, unveiling the secrets of stillness, the whispers of purpose, and the inner fortitude of the invincible mariner. Like the dyer who colors his cloth not by a hurried dip but by a sustained immersion, we too shall immerse ourselves in the wisdom that silence offers, dying our character in hues of tranquility, purpose, and resilience. Here, in the serene depths of our being, lies the power to maintain an unyielding focus amidst life's distractions. Set sail, then, for it is in this silence that we encounter the very essence of our existence.

Just as the depths of the ocean remain undisturbed by the tempestuous dance of the waves above, we too must cultivate an inner realm of silence and tranquility, an unwavering sanctuary amidst the ceaseless whirl of existence. This is the art of stillness. It is not an escape from the tumultuous torrents of life, but a steadfast anchorage that provides perspective, clarity, and serene endurance.

We are often swept up by the torrents of external happenings, tossed on the wild sea of the world's noise. The urgent tasks, the enthralling spectacles, the hollow cries for fame or wealth—these are the sirens that tempt us into relinquishing our peace, luring us into the tumultuous waters where serenity is drowned under their deafening cacophony.

Yet remember, we are not mere leaves adrift on a river, helpless against its currents. Rather, we hold the oars with which we may steer our own course. The external world may foist its noise upon us, but it is we who hold the power to let it echo within or to mute its dissonance.

To cultivate the art of stillness, we must perceive life not as an external spectacle that commands our reactions but as an internal drama where we hold the script. The world merely presents its offerings; it is we who decide their value, their impact. The bird's song, the thunder's roar, the lover's whisper, the foe's insult—they are all alike until we impart them with meaning.

In the quest for tranquility, we must learn to let go of the desire to control the uncontrollable. The sun will rise and set, seasons will come and go, and the winds of fortune will shift as they please. However, the tranquil mind, like an unwavering rock amidst the raging sea, remains undisturbed. For it knows, that while it cannot dictate the ebb and flow of the tides, it can master its own position.

The silence we seek is not merely the absence of sound but the quieting of the mind. A mind cluttered with worries, anxieties, and endless thoughts is like a stormy sky, where the serenity of the stars is hidden behind clouds of tumultuous thoughts. The quiet mind, however, is like a clear night, where each thought is a visible star, providing guidance rather than creating chaos.

Let us learn then, not to silence our thoughts outright, but to give them their due place. To recognize them, examine them, and let them pass, like clouds drifting across the sky. Our thoughts and feelings are not our masters, but our informants. They deliver their message and we decide the response. They knock upon the door, but we decide whether to invite them in.

By mastering this art of stillness, we cultivate a silence that sings with wisdom, a tranquility that is active rather than passive. It is the harmony of a mind at peace with itself, undisturbed by the world's discord, and tuned to the melodious rhythm of nature. It is the stillness of a mind that does not shun the world, but engages with it wisely, not carried away by its noise, but dancing gracefully with its music.

For the tranquil mind knows that the world's noise is a mere distraction from the symphony of existence. And in the art of stillness, we learn to hear this grand symphony, playing the melodies of wisdom and harmony that guide us on our journey through life. So, harness your mind, steer it with wisdom, let it find tranquility amidst the cacophony. Be the serene ocean beneath the storm, be the master of your inner symphony. For within you, in the grand silence, exists the most profound music of all: the melody of a life lived with purpose, clarity, and unyielding peace.

In the bustling agora of existence, myriad voices clamor for our attention, like the din of competing vendors. Amidst this cacophony, there exists a voice of singular importance, soft yet unwavering, delicate yet resonant. It is not a voice heard with our ears, but felt with our spirit. It does not shout above the crowd but waits patiently for the quietude of a receptive mind. This is the Voice of Purpose, the silent guide that, when heeded, steers us unerringly towards our true destiny.

The Voice of Purpose is not an intruder in our consciousness. It does not force itself upon our awareness, rather, it is the echo of our deepest self, the most authentic embodiment of who we are. In every human breast, there beats a heart that yearns for expression, and in every mind, there dwells a purpose seeking its path.

Yet, it is not uncommon for us to miss this gentle whisper. The world, with its enchanting diversions and vivid spectacles, lures us away from the center of our being. We become absorbed in the play of shadows, forgetting that we too are actors with roles of our own. Engrossed in the scenes of others, we neglect the script of our own play, written not in ink but in the spirit of our unique purpose.

We may ask, how does one distinguish the Voice of Purpose from the clamor of the world? It is not by volume, for the most insistent voices are often those of distraction. It is not by persistence, for the incessant drone of the world seldom ceases. No, it is by the resonance that it strikes within us, the inner harmony that it evokes, that we discern the call of purpose amidst life's distractions.

Yet, understanding this voice is but one step of the journey. The world is like a torrential river, and we, the swimmers. To reach the shores of purpose, we must not only hear its call but also possess the courage and resolve to swim against the current. Our purpose is not always aligned with the flow of the world. More often than not, it commands us to tread the uncharted path, to break new ground where none dared before.

Just as the master sculptor chisels away the excess stone to reveal the masterpiece within, we must learn to eliminate the distractions that cloud our clarity. And what are these distractions but judgments, external and self-imposed, that we imbue with more power than they truly possess? One must learn to use the hammer of discernment and the chisel of wisdom to free oneself from the fetters of judgment.

Consider not the noise of the world as an enemy, but as the backdrop against which the symphony of your purpose can be discerned. In the stillness of the mind, the voice that persistently seeks to guide you towards your true path becomes apparent. Practice silencing the external cacophony not by plugging your ears, but by learning to listen deeply to the voice within.

The Voice of Purpose is not a raucous dictator, but a gentle guide. It is a beacon that shines amidst life's tempests, providing a point of reference when the way seems lost. By focusing on it, we can steer our ship towards the safe harbors of self-fulfillment.

The road to purpose is not a well-trodden path, but a journey across unexplored landscapes. Yet, the compass of purpose, once understood and embraced, can guide us with unerring accuracy. To listen to it requires courage, to follow it demands resilience, but to live in harmony with it brings a fulfillment that surpasses all worldly pursuits.

So, dear reader, amidst the clamor and clamoring of

existence, I urge you to still your mind, focus your heart, and listen. The Voice of Purpose is speaking, guiding you towards the life you were meant to live. It may be a whisper now, but in that whisper lies the power to roar. Listen, and let it lead you towards the fulfillment of your highest potential.

It is in the nature of the sea to churn and storm; likewise, it is in the nature of life to present us with trials and tribulations. But let us not blame the sea for its waves, nor life for its storms. They are but performing their roles in the grand ballet of existence. It falls upon us, not to still the sea, but to learn the art of sailing through its billows with resolute focus and unwavering purpose.

Consider, if you will, the mariner. He embarks on a journey knowing well the capriciousness of the seas. Does he fear the tempest or curse the winds? No. He accepts these as intrinsic to his voyage. He neither dreads the storm nor prays for perpetual calm. Instead, he readies his ship, tightens his sails, and holds firm his course.

In the mariner's endeavor, we glimpse a profound wisdom. The storm he faces is not outside, but within. External circumstances are much like the winds and waves, they merely propose a direction, but it is the set of our sails, our decisions and actions, which determine our course.

Now, consider your own life. Much like the mariner, you too are on a voyage. Your ship, your being, is constantly buffeted by winds of change, waves of uncertainty, and undercurrents of doubt. The world outside is a shifting panorama of scenes, an ever-changing tapestry woven with the threads of circumstance. And, like the sea, it is often indifferent to your struggles or desires.

In this grand odyssey, the helm of choice is your greatest instrument. It is this helm that lets you navigate through storms of adversity and currents of change. The tempests of life, however fierce, are impotent against the mariner who masters his helm. Remember, it is not the violence of the winds but the deftness of your navigation that determines your journey's end.

Hence, maintain your focus on the task at hand, and you remain the master of your vessel, however roiled the seas. Like the seasoned mariner, see every storm not as a menace, but as a teacher. Let the winds of circumstance fill your sails, but let the compass of your purpose chart your course.

Distractions, fears, and desires are but sirens singing seductively from the isles of illusion. Pay them no heed. Instead, listen to the silent song of your true self, the indomitable spirit within. Do not fear to venture into the uncharted waters of the present. Every moment navigated with purpose and presence brings you closer to the shores of your dreams.

Staying focused on your current actions and decisions is akin to tightening your grasp on the helm. The waves may thrash, and the winds may howl, but your ship will hold its course. As the master of your voyage, understand that you have no dominion over the sea but complete control over your ship.

Each action, each decision, is a turn of the helm, a minor adjustment that, over time, steers your journey towards its destined harbor. Let your hands remain steady, your gaze unyielding, and your heart braced against the storm. Then, you will find that no tempest is too formidable, no wave too overwhelming, for you are the invincible mariner, sailing steadfastly on the sea of life.

CHAPTER 5: DREAMS AND REALITY

Dreams stand as majestic pillars, guiding us towards our higher calling. Each dream is like a North Star, shining brightly, offering a beacon of hope amidst the tumultuous storms of life.

However, dreams are not birthed in the gossamer threads of idle fancy nor are they sculpted in the fleeting clouds of wishful thinking. Like gold veined within the earth, they are hidden within the dense rock of reality, waiting to be unearthed by those possessing the right tools: courage, persistence, and, above all, unyielding focus.

True dreams, those worthy of our pursuit, are not vague illusions dangled on the horizon of tomorrow. Rather, they are silent whispers urging us towards a higher self, a self we begin to mold here, in the furnace of the present.

We are not the passive observers of our dreams. In the present, we become the artists and our dreams the marble. The chisel we wield is our focus, the strokes are our actions, and every moment presents an opportunity to shape that marble. With every act grounded in the now, we remove a nonessential piece, slowly revealing the masterpiece that lies within.

And what of reality, you ask? Reality is the canvas upon which our dreams take shape. It is the anvil against which we hammer our purpose, the loom whereupon the threads of our dreams intertwine to form the tapestry of our lives.

Our task then is not to shun reality, not to seek refuge in the misty lands of escapism. No, we must dance with reality. Like a skilled potter shaping clay, we must embrace it, understand its rhythm, and use its very substance to mold our dreams into existence.

Dreams are not an escape from reality, but a dialogue with it. They are the bridge between the realm of possibility and the world of actuality, a bridge we construct in the unceasing now. A wise person does not shun reality or wish for it to be other than what it is, instead, they use reality as the ultimate tool, as the raw material for the manifestation of their dreams.

In this chapter, we shall explore this interplay of

dreams and reality. The journey ahead requires of us courage, resilience, and unwavering focus. In return, it promises a life molded by our hands, a life in which our dreams no longer flutter in the realm of imagination but stand firm in the arena of reality.

Therefore, let us proceed, bearing in mind that it is not merely about reaching the destination, but about the wisdom, character, and insight we gain from the journey. For dreams are not merely about the future we want to create, but about the individuals we aspire to become in the process. And this becoming, this grand metamorphosis, it unfolds here and now, within the crucible of the present.

DREAMS AS NORTH STARS

As we traverse the boundless expanse of existence, our dreams serve as our North Stars, illuminating the otherwise opaque canvas of our lives. These dreams, whether they be of virtuous deeds, attainment of wisdom, or accomplishment of meaningful endeavors, serve as celestial points of reference. They guide us through the daunting night of uncertainty and lend us a sense of direction amidst the swirling gusts of distraction.

Yet, we must not confuse these guiding stars with the firm ground on which we tread. For the stars, though they shine brightly, are distant, and we do not inhabit them. We live, breathe, act, and shape our destiny here, in the material domain of the present. This realm, this very moment, is where the essence of our existence is distilled.

We gaze upon the stars, but we walk the earth. In this humble dichotomy lies the practical wisdom of life. The lofty grandeur of dreams pulls us upwards, yet it is the strength of our steps, measured and intentional, that propels us forward. A dream, no matter how noble or grand, is but an illusion if we do not walk towards it in the reality of the present.

Consider the humble seeds lying dormant beneath the winter's frost, dreaming of blossoming into vibrant flowers. Yet they do not yearn futilely for the warmth of spring while the world is still gripped by winter's chill. They understand the rhythm of existence, the necessity of patience. When the warmth of spring does return, they do not waste it dreaming of the autumn harvest. Instead, they seize the present, embracing the sun and the rain, pushing through the soil to extend their verdant reach towards the sky.

Dreams are not fulfilled merely by dreaming, but by the actions we undertake in each living, breathing moment. Each step we take in the reality of now is a step towards the dream that hovers like a beacon in the distance. Each moment lived with conscious intention is a moment that brings our dream closer to our lived reality.

Be like the mariner who, guided by the North Star, nevertheless remains mindful of the immediate sea and the current gust of wind. Navigate the sea of existence with an unwavering focus on the task at hand, allowing the distant glow of your dreams to guide your journey.

However, the disciplined mind understands this:

dreams are not the masters that whip us into relentless pursuit, but the companions that accompany us, inspiring us towards virtuous actions. Like the seasoned mariner knows the capricious nature of the sea, yet does not abandon his voyage, we too must acknowledge that the stars may shift, the dreams may evolve. Our task is not to chain ourselves to a dream, but to the virtues and efforts that lead to its realization.

Be like the archer, whose aim is not merely to hit the target, but to shoot well. For the outcome is not always in our control, but the integrity and focus of our actions always are.

The one who understands this intricate dance between dreams and actions holds the key to serenity amidst life's turbulence. He dreams, yet does not become a slave to his dreams. He acts, but his actions are not frantic efforts to seize control of the future, rather they are conscious engagements with the present. He treats dreams as his guiding stars, not as distant lands to conquer.

In our dreams lie the blueprint of our potential, the echo of our authentic self. In our actions, we realize this potential. So dream, fellow traveler, but do not lose yourself in the dream. Stay rooted in the present, and let each action be a conscious step towards the star that lights your path. Let your dreams be your compass, your actions the winds, and your unwavering focus the steadfast mariner, navigating the vast sea of existence.

The stage of life is set with a rhythm all its own, a rhythm born of natural law and the interplay of cause and effect. It is a dance, one that thrives in the now, in the vibrant heart of reality. Too often, we seek to impose our tempo upon this dance, thrusting against the world in a futile attempt to bend it to our will. Yet, this is akin to wrestling with the river's flow or commanding the wind to alter its course.

Reality, you see, does not bow to the whims of the un-willing dancer. Instead, it invites us to understand its rhythm, to listen to its cadence and learn its steps. It is in this under-standing, in this harmonious movement with what is, that we find the freedom to truly dance.

Indeed, there is an art to this dance with reality, one which calls for the clarity of perception, the acceptance of the present, and the flexibility to adjust our steps. This dance, my friend, is not won by force but by fluidity. It is not a battle to be waged but a waltz to be embraced.

Consider the reed in the wind. It does not resist the gusts; it bends with them. It does not break; it sways. It stands firm in its roots, yet flexible in its stance, its dance a harmonious acceptance of the forces that move it. This is the wisdom we must take to heart.

When reality presents a storm, we should not vainly shout at the winds but adjust our sails. When reality brings a night, we should not curse the darkness, but learn to dance under the stars. It is not the events of life that define our journey, but our reactions to them, our dance steps if you will.

Dance then, not against reality, but with it. Do not meet force with force; meet it with understanding. Let your steps be not of resistance, but of harmony. Embrace the rhythm of now, the melody of the moment. Make of it your own music.

Every moment is a step in this dance. Every breath, every beat of our hearts, is a note in the symphony of existence. When we fight against reality, we create discord. But when we learn to dance with it, we create music.

Your dreams, those stars you aspire to reach, are not separate from this dance. They are a part of it. They are the music you are composing with your life. You will not reach them by stumbling against the rhythm of reality but by flowing with it. Your dreams are not in some distant future; they are being danced into existence in the reality of the present moment.

You have been granted a tremendous gift: the chance to partake in the grand dance of existence. You are not a mere observer; you are a participant. And in this dance, there are no wrong steps, only lessons. Each misstep is an opportunity to learn, to adjust, to better understand the rhythm of reality.

So I beseech you, surrender not to despair when your steps falter. Instead, allow the music of reality to guide your movements. Listen to its rhythm, move with its flow. Your dreams are not the destination of this dance, but its very essence. They are realized not in the fight against what is, but in the embrace of it.

Dance, then, with reality. Let your steps be a testament to your acceptance, your strength, and your resilience. And in the rhythm of the now, in the cadence of the present, may you find the melody of your dreams.

In this great forge we call existence, our dreams are the raw material, awaiting transformation. They start as nebulous visions, much like the iron ore pulled from the heart of the earth, untamed and unshaped. The fervor of our dreams heats this iron, but it is in the searing fires of the present moment that the malleability of dreams is truly revealed. Only in this scorching crucible can the raw ore of dreams be turned into the steel of reality.

The present moment is our anvil. It is here that the hammer of our will meets the hot iron of our dreams. Each stroke, each decision, and each action shapes the pliable substance of our dreams. Over time, the ore begins to yield, slowly taking the form of our vision.

How often do we lose ourselves in the fog of the future, seeking in its nebulous depths the crystallized form of our dreams? But the future is an enigma, a shifting mirage that eludes the grasp of certainty. It is a journeyman's folly to expect the anvil of the present to reside in the yet-to-come. We must remember that the future is but the unborn child of the present. It is in the now, in the womb of the present, where we can truly nurture and shape our dreams.

Let us reflect on the role of the blacksmith, a role we must adopt in the creation of our reality. When he forges a tool, he does not aimlessly pound upon the heated metal, lost in thoughts of the object it might someday become. Instead, he immerses himself wholly in the present, each hammer stroke a focused expression of his intent. With each beat upon the glowing iron, the smith does not gaze into the future; he observes the metal as it bends and forms in the here and now.

We must follow in his method. For the blacksmith knows, as we should, that the tool's final form is not a creation of the future, but an accumulation of the present moments. With every decisive strike, he brings the vision of the tool closer to reality. The blacksmith's hammer does not fall in the future, nor does it fall in the past. It falls now, and it is the echo of these continuous 'nows' that will resonate as the clear chime of a dream realized.

One may argue, then, that the future is only the echo of our present actions, reverberating through the corridor of time. To let our focus dwell in the foggy uncertainty of the future is akin to the blacksmith swinging his hammer in the air, hoping to shape the metal without contact. It is not the future that shapes our dreams; it is the persistent hammering in the unyielding now.

As we navigate life's vast ocean, let us not be sailors who, obsessed with distant horizons, neglect the handling of their vessel. It is not the horizon that carries us forward, but the winds caught in our sails. These winds are our actions and decisions, blowing in the ever-recurring gust of now. Let us, then, attend to our sails and steer in the direction of our dreams.

The anvil of the present awaits your hammer. The reality of your dreams is born in the heart of these continuous moments. Let the echoes of your purposeful strikes fill the forge of existence, announcing to the world, with resounding clarity, the creation of your dream. Make not a leap into the fog of the future, but a step into the clear light of the present. For it is in this unyielding now, upon the anvil of reality, that dreams are transformed into existence.

CHAPTER 6: THE MARATHON OF LIFE

As we tread the path of existence, we must remember, dear reader, that life does not engage in sprints; it is a marathon of unceasing transformation and unending discovery. In the grand spectacle of the cosmos, the swift hares may shine brightly for a brief moment, but it is the patient tortoises who, step by measured step, trace a path towards wisdom and fulfillment.

Our ambitions and aspirations, the shining stars in our personal firmament, do not fall upon us in an instantaneous shower of golden realization. Rather, they descend slowly, often imperceptibly, crafted and honed in the crucible of our steadfast focus and unwavering resolve.

In this grand marathon, the landscapes of our journey are rarely static, but a shifting tableau of experience, each day birthing new scenery. From the sunlit plains of prosperity to the shadowed valleys of adversity, every stretch of this terrain shapes and strengthens us, adding another stroke to the canvas of our character. Yet, no matter the terrain, the truly resilient runner does not waste breath cursing the uneven path or decrying the length of the journey. Instead, they focus on each footfall, each heartbeat echoing in the present moment, for that is the only domain where the race is truly run.

This understanding, however, should not dishearten us, but rather, illuminate the magnificence of our existence. As a potter slowly forms a lump of clay into a work of art, so do we mold our lives through countless decisions, one moment at a time. The grandeur of our dreams is not found in the swiftness of their realization but in the steady and purposeful pursuit of them.

So, let us not lament over the length of the road, or the weight of the burdens we carry. Let us instead celebrate the strength that carries us forward, the wisdom that guides us, and the focus that illuminates our path. Remember, we are not simply subject to the marathon of life, we are its participants, its artists. Every step, every breath, every heartbeat is a testament to our agency, a silent affirmation of our indomitable spirit.

In the end, it is not about reaching the finish line faster than others, but about understanding the race itself, embracing its challenges, savoring its triumphs, and learning from its lessons. Only then can we say we have truly run the marathon of life.

And so, dear reader, let us delve into the profound intricacies of this marathon, as we explore the means to sustain our focus, the art of weathering uncertainties, and the joy of witnessing our dreams take shape in the crucible of the present.

Life is a race, though it would be folly to imagine it as a sprint, a fleeting dash towards some glittering finish line. Life, my dear reader, is not won in short, frenzied bursts of energy, but in the long, enduring journey that we often term as a marathon.

Imagine a master sculptor, laboring day and night, ceaselessly chipping away at the insurmountable block of marble. Does he dream of an immediate masterpiece, or does he perceive the gradual emergence of form, the slow revelation of beauty beneath the hardened exterior? Indeed, each strike of the chisel, each grain of dust that falls away, is a step forward on the path to eventual perfection.

Our dreams, too, are much like this marble block. We start with a vision, but the materialization of that vision takes not mere moments, but a lifetime of dedication, a lifetime of concentrated focus and relentless effort.

It is not the dreamer who reclines in the shade of expectation who manifests his dreams, but the doer who bares himself to the harsh winds of reality. It is the one who labors in the heat of the day, whose hands bear the scars of unrelenting effort, who ultimately molds his dreams into reality. He knows that the path to success is long and winding, that it meanders through valleys of despair and over mountains of uncertainty. Yet, he perseveres.

Therein lies the crucial understanding: dreams do not suddenly manifest out of the ether of wishful thinking. They are born from the womb of time, nurtured by the nourishing milk of relentless action, and reared under the stern discipline of patience.

The world with its transitory pleasures and pain, whispers in our ears, beckoning us to rest, to enjoy the distractions that present themselves. It can be tempting to forsake our journey, to be carried away by these ephemeral delights or to become overwhelmed by the trials. But to halt is to surrender your dream to the cruel hands of oblivion. To divert is to sacrifice the worthy on the altar of the unworthy.

A wise man said that we are but actors on the stage of life, each handed a role to play. Let us, then, not wish for easy parts but strive to play our given roles well, even if they are long and demanding.

Your role, dear reader, is to dream and to make those

dreams a reality. It is a lengthy script, filled with lines of failure and moments of despair. But as you read further, you'll also find scenes of triumph, and the final act is one of victory, a victory born from consistency, focus, and indomitable spirit.

Let the sprinters have their fleeting moments of glory, for as the torchbearer of your dreams, you are destined for a greater journey. You run a marathon. A marathon towards the actualization of your purpose. The finish line may seem distant, shrouded in the mist of time. Yet, remember, with each step, each drop of sweat, you are forging your destiny. Let this understanding fuel your run, steady your breath, and strengthen your stride.

In the relentless pursuit of dreams, patience must be your closest ally, and time, your humble servant. With these companions, the long and winding road shall become a glorious journey, and in due time, the marathon runner shall reap the laurels of steadfast endurance, persistence, and unyielding focus. You will arrive, not because you traveled swiftly, but because you traveled surely, and did not halt until the journey was done.

In this light, dear reader, gird yourself for the long

run. Embrace the marathon of life. For in the steady rhythm of enduring progress, your dreams will slowly, but surely, transform from mere sparks in your mind to a glorious blaze in reality.

It is inevitable that we will find ourselves on roads obscured by the mists of uncertainty. They swirl around us, cloaking our surroundings in an opaque veil, transforming the familiar into the unknown. Such circumstances are not to be feared, but to be approached as part of the natural ebb and flow of existence.

Just as the wise mariner navigates the sea through dense fog, we too must learn to steer through the misty paths of life. The mariner relies not on sight but on a deep understanding of his craft and a trust in the rhythm of the sea. Similarly, we are called to navigate the shadows of uncertainty with the compass of our virtues and the steady pulse of patience.

Uncertainty, while initially disorienting, is not an adversary, but an instructor. It is a teacher that does not provide answers, but inspires questions. It does not bring comfort, but provokes growth. Uncertainty is a forge, in which the character of a man is tested, purified, and ultimately strengthened.

Patience, then, is the helm we must grip firmly amidst

the gloom. It is not a passive resignation to circumstance, but an active cultivation of endurance. Just as the river, unhurried, carves its path through the mountains, patience enables us to shape our destiny amidst the dense fog of confusion. It tempers our spirit, allowing us to continue forward, one step at a time, when our goal is concealed by life's uncertainties.

In the heart of patience is the understanding that we control not the unfolding of events around us, but our responses to them. It is here, in the misty, unclear paths, that we truly grasp the essence of this truth. We may not have the power to dispel the fog or illuminate the path, but we can choose how to tread upon it.

Let us then, adopt the temperament of the stoic mariner. Rather than cursing the mist, he adjusts his sails, checks his compass, and moves forward with resolute confidence. The mist does not concern him. He knows it will lift in due time, and until then, he does not suspend his journey, but continues with unwavering focus.

In these obscured paths, let us remember that the value of our journey is not merely in reaching our destination, but in the wisdom we acquire and the person we become en route. Each moment of confusion is an invitation to deepen our understanding, to fine-tune our instincts, and to reinforce our resolve. The misty path is not a barrier, but a crucible for the stoic mind, a place where focus and patience become steadfast guides leading us to a clarity borne not of sight, but of insight.

So, when the fog of uncertainty surrounds you, hold steadfast to the helm of patience, keep your focus sharp, and remember that every step taken with conscious intent brings you closer to your destination. The fog is temporary, but the wisdom gleaned from navigating it, enduring in its influence, will serve as a beacon of guidance in all future travels. The mists of uncertainty are, in truth, the unseen teachers of the stoic traveler, gifting lessons of resilience, patience, and focused perseverance.

The Unveiling Tapestry

Our lives are akin to a tapestry being woven. Each thread represents a moment, each stitch a choice, and the pattern that gradually unveils itself forms the narrative of our lives. In its totality, it is overwhelming, chaotic even. Yet, if we turn our gaze to a single stitch, a single thread, it becomes discernible, manageable. Therein lies the secret - not in attempting to see the full pattern all at once, but in focusing on each individual stitch, each individual thread.

Our dreams, those lustrous stars in our personal firmament, may seem distant, shrouded in the veils of the yet-to-come. However, it is crucial to remember that they are not located in some remote future but are in fact rooted in the present. They manifest through the choices we make, the actions we take in each living moment.

Like the patient weaver who focuses on every thread, who stays present with every stitch, so must we learn to live. We should not be dissuaded by the vastness of the tapestry nor should we be entranced by the shimmer of the completed pattern. It is the single thread under our fingers, the single stitch that the needle is making, that should hold our complete attention.

Imagine the cart-horse, yoked to a heavy burden. Does it distress itself over the length of the journey ahead? No. It focuses on the ground immediately before it, taking one step at a time. It understands, in its humble wisdom, that it is the aggregation of these individual steps, these present moments, that accomplishes the journey. Similarly, we must remind ourselves that the path to our dreams is traversed not in leaps and bounds, but in mindful steps, stitched one at a time in the fabric of now.

Every moment is a battlefield where our focus wrestles with distractions. Every decision is a crucible wherein our present choices shape our future reality. Every action is a thread, and with mindfulness and diligence, we weave it into our life's tapestry. In surrendering to the illusion of distance and time, we place our dreams on a pedestal far removed from our present reality. The philosopher's wisdom teaches us that this is folly. It encourages us to see that our dreams are not separated from us by a chasm of time but are merely the sum of our present moments lived with intention and focus.

The key to unveiling the tapestry of our dreams lies

in our hands, not in some distant tomorrow. By focusing on the thread of the present, by stitching with a clear mind and a resolute heart, we gradually weave the grand pattern of our dreams.

Take heed, then, not to disperse your energies between the ephemeral past and the nebulous future. Draw them instead into the crucible of the present. With each focused stitch, each mindful decision, each purposeful action, you bring your dreams closer into your reality. Remember that the realization of dreams is not an event but a process, a steady unveiling, one stitch at a time, in the unyielding loom of the present.

Steadfast in your purpose, patient in your progress, your tapestry will come to life, thread by thread, moment by moment. The dreams you once believed were distant stars will descend to become the threads in your hands, and you will find them woven into the fabric of your existence. For it is in the journey, not the destination, that the pattern of life reveals itself. Embrace the power of the present and watch as the unveiling tapestry of your dreams transforms from an ethereal vision into a tangible reality.

CONCLUSION
RECAP OF KEY INSIGHTS

We have traversed an expanse of wisdom and understanding in the realm of focus and presence. The pathway of knowledge we've embarked upon is not one of linearity, but rather an unending spiral where we repeatedly revisit the core tenets, each time with a deeper perception and more profound wisdom.

We commenced our journey in the arena of distractions, that ceaseless whirlwind of external influences that attempt to sway us from our steadfast purpose. The world sings a cacophonous symphony, a melody woven with threads of fear, regret, anticipation, and uncertainty. In the face of this noise, we are compelled to recollect the inherent power of silence, the serene sea that lies within us, and the potent voice of purpose that emerges from this stillness.

The quintessence of our exploration has been a reassessment of time and our relation to it. We have unearthed the futility of dwelling in the past, an echo chamber reverberating with what has been, and the folly of being consumed by the future, an illusory landscape painted by the brushstrokes of speculation and dread. This book has been an homage to the present, a silent hymn to the potent power of now. Our power lies neither in the tomb of past actions nor in the womb of future anxieties, but in the womb of the present moment, where dreams are conceived and nurtured.

We have learnt to stand firmly on the deck of the present, our eyes not affixed on the receding shoreline of the past or the unseen horizons of the future, but on the swelling wave of the present moment. We have understood that the tempests of life do not define us, it is how we navigate through them that carves our character. The storm tests not the strength of the sea but the mettle of the sailor. In each moment of turbulence, we are presented with a choice: to be swept away by the storm or to harness the winds of adversity to fill our sails.

In the pursuit of our dreams, we have discovered the dance of reality. The present moment is the only stage on which this dance unfolds, and our focus, the steps with which we move. There is an art to dancing with reality, a skill in marrying our intentions with the rhythm of the universe. It is not a fight against what is, but an acceptance and a willful act of engaging with the present in all its raw, unfiltered essence.

Let us not be disillusioned into thinking that the journey to our dreams is a swift sprint. It is a marathon that tests not only our strength but our endurance. It is a path shrouded in mist and uncertainty. Yet it is within this uncertainty that our focused intent becomes the torchlight illuminating our steps. We move not with reckless haste but with measured strides, always grounded in the immediate step, the task at hand.

All this wisdom is not a mere accumulation of intellectual understanding, but a call to enact these insights in the theatre of our lives. Let it not be forgotten that the words of wisdom are futile if they do not permeate our actions. Theory, when met with practice, becomes wisdom, a beacon illuminating our path. Therefore, as we tread the path towards our dreams, let our focus be as steady as the unwavering flame, our presence as rooted as the ancient tree, and our resolve as unyielding as the relentless river carving its path through the mountains.

In this conclusion, we weave together these threads of insight into a tapestry of wisdom, yet know this: understanding is the beginning, not the end. The book may be closing, but the journey continues. For it is not the knowing of the path, but the walking of it, that turns dreams into reality. And on this path, may the present moment be your faithful guide, and focused intent, your trusted companion.

The Stoic's Final Word

You, my fellow traveler, have found yourself poised at the precipice of understanding, at the threshold of a new dawn. As your feet tread the path of the Stoic, a path chiseled with the fortitude of unyielding focus, it becomes necessary to pause, to reflect, and to prepare for the journey ahead.

To foster unyielding focus and an unwavering presence in each moment is to command the helm of a ship coursing through the sea of existence. Storms will come, as is their nature. Waves will rise, as is their duty. Your task, like that of a seasoned mariner, is not to silence the tempest, but to hold firm your course, navigating through life's gales with an eye as steady as the North Star.

This, the art of focus and presence, is akin to the taming of a wild horse. Much like the untrained steed, the unmastered mind gallops aimlessly through the fields of distraction. But the skillful rider, harnessing the beast's power with a firm yet gentle hand, finds his stride in harmonious synchrony with his mount. The goal then, is not to quell the horse's spirit, but to guide it, making of it not a burden, but an ally.

In the cultivation of this unwavering focus, you will find not merely a tool, but a shield and a sword. A shield against the arrows of worry shot from the bow of the future, a sword to cut through the dense thicket of regrets grown from the seeds of the past. Let your sword be sharp, your shield sturdy, and your grip unyielding.

Yet, let us not become entranced by the seductive song of eternal focus. For, just as a tightly strung bow soon breaks, so too does the mind overly strained under the yoke of ceaseless concentration. Recognize, then, that the path of the Stoic is not one of tension, but of balance. It is the balance between the potency of purposeful focus and the tranquility of accepting presence.

In this harmony, you will find yourself capable of embracing the present, each moment a droplet in the flowing river of time. Every drop holds within its translucent self the capacity for change, for action, for realization. Each moment is a stepping stone across the brook of becoming, leading you toward the far shore of your aspirations. Step with care, with awareness, for once a stone is passed, it recedes into the irretrievable depths of yesterday.

In this journey, the world will test your resolve. Distractions will call to you like sirens in the night, their melodies sweet, their promises hollow. To these alluring whispers, pay no heed. Remember, the clamor of a thousand meaningless voices cannot drown out the resonant truth of a single focused thought.

Do not falter in your dedication to the now, do not waver in your pursuit of undivided focus. To walk this path is not merely to dream, but to wake up within the dream, to understand that the shaping of our reality happens here, in the now, under the patient and watchful eye of focus.

And thus, my fellow voyager, it is with these final words I leave you. Carry them close to your heart as you would a cherished amulet. As you traverse the seas of life, may you steer with wisdom, navigate with focus, and journey with presence, until, guided by the North Star of your dreams, you reach the welcoming shores of your destiny.

It is in the nature of wisdom not merely to be heard, but to be absorbed and enacted. For wisdom is the seed and action is the fertile soil in which it germinates. If we take a moment to reflect, we realize that all words, no matter how profound, are mere gusts of wind if they do not instigate action. They float about in the ether, void of substance, devoid of meaning.

The lessons laid out before you are not meant to be mere objects of contemplation, but catalysts for transformation. Like the blacksmith who shapes his steel under the relentless hammer and unyielding flame, you too must subject yourself to the forge of action to shape your being. The lessons contained within these pages yearn to be tried and tested in the crucible of life's trials, to emerge hardened, gleaming, and true.

This invitation, dear reader, is for you to breathe life into these principles, to bring them into the tangible world from the realm of ideas. It is not enough to understand the value of the present moment, one must live in it. Not merely to appreciate the importance of focus, but to wield it as the master artist uses his brush, imbuing each stroke with intention and precision.

The tapestry of your life awaits your hand. Each moment is a thread, and with focus, you can weave them into a masterpiece. Yet, remember, a weaver must work with the threads they hold now, not the ones they used yesterday or the ones they hope to use tomorrow.

In your voyage across the sea of life, let not the waves of distraction carry you off course. Equip yourself with the compass of the present, let your rudder be guided by the winds of purposeful action, and let your sails be filled with the gusts of unwavering focus.

Do not become a mere spectator of your existence. Seize the reins of your life firmly. Recall the wisdom of the great charioteer who once said, "It's not what happens to you, but how you react to it that matters." Let this reminder be your shield as you march forward, meeting each challenge not with dread, but with focused resolve.

Do not merely read these words. Live them. Breathe them. Act upon them. Each day is a fresh canvas. Paint upon it with the vibrant colors of presence and focus. Let the world be your arena, your actions the valiant gladiator, and these principles the skills that guide your combat. Engage with life not as a timid observer but as a passionate participant.

Understand, however, that this path is not laden with roses. It is a strenuous journey, fraught with challenges. At times, you may falter, your focus may waver, and you may lose sight of the present. Yet remember, it is the arduous uphill path that leads to the breathtaking summit. Embrace the journey with all its vicissitudes.

And when your focus falters, let it not be a cause for despair. Instead, let it serve as a reminder, a call back to the present moment. For even in the heart of winter, the tree stands resolute, not bemoaning the falling leaves but readying itself for the bloom of spring.

Take these words, not as mere suggestions, but as commands to the soul. Commands that urge you to plunge into the vibrant sea of life with an unwavering gaze and an unyielding spirit. For it is in this very engagement, this dance with the present, that the tapestry of your dreams will unravel, and the true spectacle of life will unfold.

The art of life awaits your hand. Take the chisel of focus, and on the marble of the present, sculpt your destiny.

Be the master of your moments, and the shaper of your dreams. In the theater of existence, let not your life be a mere echo, but a resonant voice that adds to the symphony of the cosmos. As the sun rises tomorrow, begin anew. Live in the present. Focus. Act. And let the transformation begin.

Printed in Great Britain
by Amazon

26767870R00052